I Wonder if
GEORGE WASHINGTON
Owned a Pooper Scooper?

Written by Jen Walkington   Illustrated by David W. Hinton

Published by Orange Hat Publishing 2019

ISBN 978-1-64538-004-7

Orange Hat
PUBLISHING

www.orangehatpublishing.com

From the author:

"This is for my boys, Jeff, Jackson, and Avery –
my world. I love you bigger than the sky."

From the illustrator:

"Thanks to my wife and daughters for their
encouragement and support, and especially
to Isabelle, without whom the drawings in this
book would not have been possible."

We all know that George Washington was the first President of the United States. Our country's capital is named after him, and he is called "The Father of Our Nation" because he led the United States through the American Revolution as a general in the Continental Army. He was the first leader of our brand-new country and had to decide what it meant to be a President of the United States.

But did you know . . .

He owned over 30 hound dogs, and three of them were named True Love, Vulcan, and Sweet Lips?

I wonder if George Washington owned a pooper scooper?

Thomas Jefferson was our country's 3rd President. He was a strong believer in breaking ties with Britain and forming a new colony. He was the author of the Declaration of Independence and served as a lawyer, colonel, governor of Virginia, member of Congress, Secretary of State, minister to France, and the 2nd Vice President of the United States. He was responsible for hiring Lewis and Clark to explore land in the west that he bought from France that no one in the US had been to before. It was called the Louisiana Purchase, and it doubled the size of the United States.

But did you know . . .

In Jefferson's private library, he owned over 6,000 books?

I wonder how long it took to pack all of his books when he moved into the White House?

Everyone has heard of Abraham Lincoln, our 16th President. He led the United States through the Civil War, which abolished slavery. Lincoln gave a famous speech called the Gettysburg Address, which is considered one of the greatest speeches in history. He was known as "Honest Abe" and was the first President to have a beard.

But did you know . . .

Lincoln was one of the tallest US Presidents?

I wonder if Lincoln hated shopping for pants?

Ulysses S. Grant was our country's 18th President. He served as the general-in-chief for the Union army during the Civil War and is still considered one of the greatest military leaders in history. Grant helped establish the National Park System in our country, including the very first national park, Yellowstone! He created the Department of Justice and was a huge supporter of civil rights for all US citizens.

But did you know . . .

Grant got a speeding ticket while driving a horse and buggy in Washington, D.C.?

I wonder if he got in trouble with his wife, Julia, when he got home?

Theodore Roosevelt was our country's 26th President. He doubled the number of national parks in the US and was the first American to win a Nobel Peace Prize. He helped finish construction on the Panama Canal, which connected the Atlantic and Pacific Oceans and made shortcuts for trading. He even has his face carved into Mount Rushmore!

But did you know . . .

His whole family owned wooden stilts and walked around the White House grounds on them?

I wonder if the Roosevelts helped trim the trees on the South Lawn on the weekends?

William Taft was our country's 27th President. He was called "Big Bill" since he was the largest of the US Presidents, and he even had a special bathtub put into the White House that was big enough for him. Taft served as the Chief of Justice in the Supreme Court, which makes him the only President to serve as the head of two branches of government. He even swore in two other Presidents (Calvin Coolidge and Herbert Hoover)! He was the first President to own a car and converted the White House stables into a garage.

But did you know . . .

When he was young, Taft took dance lessons?

I wonder if Taft could tap dance?

Herbert Hoover was our country's 31st President. While he was serving as President, the United States started to experience the Great Depression, a period when a lot of people were out of work and struggled to live day-to-day. He hated to see anyone go hungry and was nominated five times for a Nobel Peace Prize for his work to help starving people all over the world. During his presidency, he donated all of his salary to charity. Hoover also signed a law that made "The Star-Spangled Banner" our country's national anthem. He even has a dam named after him (The Hoover Dam)!

But did you know . . .

Hoover's son, Allan, had two pet alligators that wandered the White House lawn?

I wonder if Hoover had special leashes made for the alligators?

Franklin D. Roosevelt was our country's 32nd President. He was Theodore Roosevelt's fifth cousin and brought the United States through most of the Great Depression and World War II. He was elected for 4 terms, which isn't allowed anymore according to the 22nd Amendment to the Constitution. Since each term is 4 years, Roosevelt would have been President for 16 years! Sadly, he died during his last term, so he was only President for 12 years. He was the first President to appear on television and spoke the famous line, "The only thing we have to fear is fear itself."

But did you know . . .

Franklin Roosevelt was related to 11 US Presidents?

I wonder if they had pie-eating contests at family reunions?

Dwight D. Eisenhower was our country's 34th President. He served in the military during both World War I and World War II and was promoted to Supreme Allied Commander of the Armed Forces (Commander-in-Chief). During his presidency, Eisenhower established NASA and the Interstate Highway System and helped end the Korean War. Also during his presidency, he supported desegregation in public schools and helped "The Little Rock Nine" (nine African-American students from Arkansas) go to an all-white high school for the first time. While Eisenhower was President, Hawaii and Alaska were added as the 49th and 50th states, which means he was the first President of all 50 states!

But did you know . . .

Besides his nickname "Ike," he was also known as "Duckpin" because he loved bowling?

I wonder if he tried bowling in the Oval Office at the end of a stressful day?

Ronald Reagan was our country's 40th President. Before he was President, he worked as a radio announcer, became a captain in the US Army, and starred in more than 50 movies. After he served as governor of California, he was elected the President of the United States in 1980.

But did you know . . .

He also worked as a lifeguard and saved 77 people in 7 summers?

I wonder if Reagan was really good at cannonballs and belly flops?

George W. Bush was the 43rd President of the United States, a former governor of Texas, and his dad (George H.W. Bush) was the 41st President. During his presidency, the country experienced the September 11, 2001 attack as well as the destruction caused by Hurricane Katrina. Bush was a pilot in the Texas Air National Guard, was the first President to finish a marathon, and was an owner of the Texas Rangers baseball team.

But did you know . . .

He was a cheerleader in high school?

I wonder if Bush could do the splits?

Fun Presidential Facts

- Six Presidents have been named James (Madison, Monroe, Polk, Buchanan, Garfield, and Carter)

- Three US Presidents have died on the 4th of July (John Adams, Thomas Jefferson, and James Monroe).

- Andrew Jackson (7th President) fought in over 100 duels in his lifetime, mostly to defend the honor of his wife, Rachel.

- Martin Van Buren (8th President) has been said to have created the word "OK". He was also the first President to be born a United States citizen (all Presidents before him were born in the British colonies).

- Rutherford B. Hayes (19th President) was the first President to use a phone. His phone number? 1.

- James Garfield (20th President) could write using both of his hands and was believed to be able to write Latin in one hand and Greek in the other at the same time!

- Chester Arthur (21st President), known as "Elegant Arthur," owned 80 pairs of pants.

- Benjamin Harrison (23rd President) was the first President to have electricity in the White House. He was so afraid of being electrocuted that he never touched the light switches.

- Gerald Ford (38th President) held his daughter's prom at the White House.

- The White House's first website was made during Bill Clinton's presidency (42nd President) in 1994.

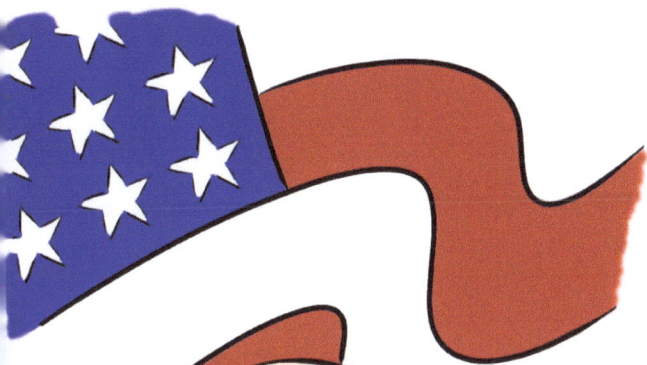

www.ingramcontent.com/pod-product-compliance
Lightning Source LLC
Chambersburg PA
CBHW042000100426
42813CB00019B/2939